# TESLA
## MAN OF MYSTERY
### BY MICHAEL X

**MANY HAVE CALLED HIM A GENIUS
BORN AHEAD OF HIS TIME
• WAS HE A WIZARD?
• DID HE COME FROM ANOTHER PLANET?
WAS HE A TIME TRAVELER FROM THE FUTURE?**

ISBN 0-938294-78-4

# TESLA
# MAN OF MYSTERY

For a complete catalog of
New Age books write to:
Inner Light Publications, Box 753,
New Brunswick, NJ 08903

Typography & design by:
Cross-Country Communications

# THE MAN WITHOUT A CENTURY

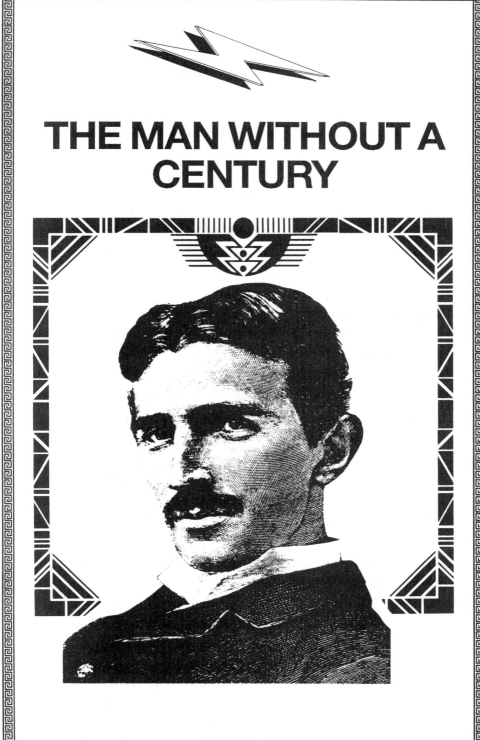

If we read the usual school textbooks, we are told we know who Nikola Tesla really was. But we are told only that he discovered the principle of alternating current (the ordinary "A.C." house current you utilize in your home). Some books may briefly sketch out some of Tesla's work in the field of static electricity, and other "conventional" fields.

What we are NOT told is that Tesla also carried out experiments and devised plans for inventions, not only "ahead of their time" in that day—but which even today would be termed "science fiction" devices by the uninitiated.

During his latter work on this plane, Tesla was secretive about most of his inventions, even to his close friends and students. It is alleged that immediately after his death, his files were seized by a certain Agency, which to this day, keeps these secrets locked away from their use by mankind, because of fears of Vested Interests that the development of these inventions might cause them economic ruin.

It is believed by many students of Tesla that this same Agency, never mentioned publicly in any publication or broadcast, is the very same one which has suppressed vital information about the presence of UFO and space people among us. Also, it is They, these students aver, who have been responsible for silencing many UFO investigators.

Perhaps we will never know who Nikola Tesla really was. Some have speculated that he was brought here as an infant from another planet, others contend that he was a mystic who based his inventions upon hunches and phantom images which constantly floated through his mind.

But whoever Nikola Tesla was he was definitely a man without a century. His discoveries, and impact on society are just today being felt.

During his lifetime he was scorned and abused by 95% of the scientific community, a community to which he felt he could help and contribute.

Whether Tesla was a spaceman or not we may probably never be able to prove. But we do know that he took an exceptional interest in the possibility of life on other planets and their future implications on our society. He even claimed to have received messages from "out there", and some of his pupils claim that he was in constant touch with interplanetary beings who were responsible for imparting some of his marvelous inventions to him by means of telepathic and verbal messages.

During the latter days of his life he was even said to have been interested in astral travel and in the possibility of life after death. And although much of this cannot be checked out we do have brief mentions of his "supernormal" interests in much of what he wrote.

The AMERICAN MAGAZINE sent a reporter to see Tesla in 1921 and he told the reporter, a Mr. M.K. Wisehart, how "During my boyhood I suffered from a particular affliction due to the appearance of images, which were often accompanied by strong flashes of light. When a word was spoken, the image of the object designated would present itself so vividly to my vision that I could not tell whether what I saw was real or not. . .Even though I reached out and passed my hand through the image, it would remain fixed in space."

Others throughout the years have written of

their experiences with Tesla but none have really been very specific when it came to the part about his interest in otherworldly communications. However one Arthur H. Matthews, now living in Canada, worked under Tesla during the time in which communications apparently were coming through on a regular basis. In fact Matthews helped construct **THE TESLA SCOPE FOR SPACE COMMUNICATION,** a diagram of which appears in print in this volume for the first time.

The information you are about to read has been communicated to me through friends on both your physical, and OTHER planes, to which I am attuned.

EXPERIMENTAL LABORATORY, COLORADO, ERECTED SUMMER OF 1899.

# AN INVENTION THAT COULD SAVE OUR PLANET

The following is a communication received from a student who has now departed the Earth Plane and who is one of the Mentors assisting advanced New Age thinkers on that Plane. This student is well known to many of our readers but is not named here for reasons we cannot reveal at this time:

In the fateful year of 1856 a space ship set out from Venus on a mission to the planet Earth. As the ship neared the earth an event took place which was to change the entire course of scientific development on this planet. A baby boy was born on board the ship, and the space people gave him the name of Nikola. At midnight, between July 9th and 10th, the space ship landed in a remote section of an Austro-Hungarian province which is today known as Yugoslavia. The child Nikola was taken to the home of a young married couple, a man and woman of goodwill, as the space people described them. The tiny Venusian prodigy was entrusted to their care—to the Rev. Milutin Tesla and his wife, Djouka. He grew up as their son, Nikola Tesla, a babe from Venus. His foster parents guarded well the secret of his birth, even when he later received worldwide recognition as Nikola Tesla, the superman. This secret has now been disclosed by the space people themselves, for they now desire that we understand more about the persons they have infiltrated into our population to aid us in our hour of need.

Tesla died in New York City during the night of January 7, 1943, and it was thought by many that his earthly work was finished. The forces of darkness rejoiced at news of his death which they considered was most opportune. The world was at war, and under pressure of this need, the patents of Tesla were considered as royal plunder. The very gifts of genius which had been intended to preserve us from wars were used to satisfy the greed, the passions, and the hatreds of the evil forces.

But darkness never wins out over Light, and now, according to the space people, the real work of Tesla is about to begin, for it is part of the Divine Plan for humanity on this earth that we enjoy in full abundance the new way of life which Tesla's inventions will bring us. Tesla was just one man, just one Venusian, who lived on this planet for 87 years. He was a scientist in the field of electrical development. Yet his inventions alone, if developed, will automatically solve every immediate need of humanity on the physical plane, leaving mankind free and at peace to develop his full soul expression.

Tesla's inventions, if developed, will make nuclear experiments obsolete; they will render warfare impossible, making each country safe within its borders, free to develop its particular culture in peace and harmony; they will open up interplanetary communication to everyone immediately; they will permit the space people to send us teachers who can train the entire population of this planet in every phase of art, philosophy, science, and Universal Law, known in this solar system. All of this and much, much more can be accomplished by the simple expedient of utilizing the inventions of Nikola Tesla.

And what can you do to further this project, this phase of the Divine Plan? You can demand, demand, demand that the inventions of Tesla be utilized. Ask and you shall receive. This is a Divine promise. Therefore, ask! Spread this word to the ends of the earth, this immediate answer to our immediate problem. If you can understand the technical aspects of these Tesla inventions, by all means study the writings on the subject, and inform yourself. But if your best efforts do not lie along scientific lines, then just seek to understand the desperate need of humanity for help in this hour, and know in your heart that help is at hand. Spread these tidings of joy!

Those of you who are yearning to see space ships in the sky, to talk to the people in those ships, to receive messages, to receive comfort, assurance, and some guarantee of security, please stop and consider. There are thousands of space people here with us now, but if you complain that you do not know any of them, that you cannot recognize them, then find comfort in the fact that Nikola Tesla of Venus was with us on this planet, in a physical body, for 87 years; he is still with us today in his subtle body. He is a practical man who has devoted his life to the greatest salvage operation that we have known on this planet since the time of Jesus. Indeed, it was Jesus Himself who said that we, in our time, would do greater things than He could do for us 2000 years ago because of our limited knowledge then.

Let us now consider just what is being done about the Tesla inventions, the attitude of the space people toward the Tesla project, and the scope of the inventions themselves.

So vast is the scientific field explored by Tesla that it is difficult to classify the work of this superman. He was not an inventor in the usual sense; he was a discoverer; the universe was his laboratory. To say that he harnessed electricity for use on a world scale is totally inadequate.

This was the man who envisioned a world-wide wireless power system, not for any one nation or group, but for all of God's children. He invented alternating current to replace the limited use of direct current, and then he harnessed Niagara Falls to supply electricity. At the age of 80 years, his wireless-power system was still to be developed, as today, but he did not resent the delay. "Perhaps I was a little premature," he said, "but meanwhile my polyphase alternating current system continues to meet our needs to lighten the burdens of mankind and increase comfort and happiness. Just as soon as the need arises I have the wireless system ready to be used with complete success."

Like the spaceman that he was, Tesla knew that he could only encourage us; he could not force his light upon us; he could only respect our free will. Nevertheless he knew that his alternating current (A.C.) system had made the power age possible, but he also knew that it had made World Wars I and II possible. Being a man of goodwill he sought to properly curb the mighty force he had unleashed in the world, so he invented, in 1935, an anti-war machine, as he called it. This anti-war machine could have been put into effect all over the world, and it would have made each country safe within its borders. It would have ended all aggression between nations. It would not have ended family and community squabbles inside national borders. . .or would it? Perhaps. Who knows what course human evolution might have taken if, say, by 1935, all fear of warfare had been removed from the world?

Remember that the space people have had vast experience in guiding other planets in other solar systems through emergencies exactly like the difficulty which faces us now. They estimate that even with their help and our unlimited cooperation, it may require about fifty years to complete the task of establishing God's kingdom on earth. They base this timing on actual results recently achieved in another solar system where the planetary problems were very similar to ours. However, they feel that we can probably progress more rapidly because we are far more developed along artistic lines, and therefore have greater imaginative and intuitive powers than our friends in the neighboring solar system.

The Tesla anti-war machine was not utilized in 1935, nor by 1955, nor at the present date; so the fear of warfare has not been removed from the world. Would you like to have the fear of warfare removed from the world now? Then go right ahead and demand your God-given heritage of human brotherhood. You can demand that human security be preserved, human dignity and human rights assured, by making all national borders secure by the installation of the Tesla anti-war machine. But your demands will have to be loud, very loud indeed, for the forces of darkness do not like to hear the sound of the voices of men and women of goodwill. Remember, too, that certain governments of the world were offered this invention of Tesla himself, away back in 1935, and his offers were spurned. Great fortunes were to be made. Nothing could interfere with that. . .nothing that is, except the voice of the people themselves. But uninformed people are silent people, and so the bloody course of history, which might have been changed, was not changed.

There is another reason why the people were not told about the anti-war machine. Tesla had invented polyphase alternating current in his youth, as a sort of stop-gap, so that people everywhere could have the immediate use of electricity, since direct current could be used only within an area of one square mile around each power station. Tesla did not intend that we should still be using an old-fashioned, complicated system of wiring and electrical distribution today. But he first had to invent a wireless method. He did this and the radio was an offshoot, a by-product of Tesla's experiments.

When he did come forward with his world wireless power system, the forces of darkness, securely entrenched behind the world's financial interests, would have none of it. One of the greatest financiers in the United States listened to Tesla himself describe the glories of his invention, and then the financier dismissed the whole subject as impractical because, as the money baron pointed out, there would be no way of making money off the people, if the people could have all the electricity they wanted by merely sticking up a little antenna on their homes, factories, or office buildings. This astute financier pointed out that under the present system the manufacturers of wires, poles, and electrical installation equipment of all kinds, could make fortunes, and in addition the electricity could be metered and everybody could be charged for every kilowatt they used.

Tesla pointed out that electricity was free in the atmosphere, a free gift of God to his people, but such idealism naturally could not penetrate the thinking of the financier.

If today we demand Tesla's invention of wireless electrical distribution, we can still have all the electricity we want by merely sticking up a little antenna on our homes and other buildings. But his is the catch. . .Tesla's anti-war machine is based on the same idea—it requires no poles, no wires, no reflectors, no platforms, no micro-wave towers, no walls or fences.

Now, if we are to have this New Age cake, we will naturally want the frosting too. This means that we can have protection along all national boundary lines without a single wall, wire, tower or any similar device. It also means that we have no further need for any kind of poles, towers, cables, reflectors or wires for electricity, telephones, telegraph, radios or television. Then, since we would have national boundary protection, and positive protection for all coasts, we could do away with the army, the navy, and the marines.

If you have doubted that Tesla was a Venusian, this is a fairly safe spot to cast aside your doubts. And if you will reflect upon this report you will realize that the space people mean business. They are collaborators with the Creator of the Universe, and when they tell us to give up warfare they mean for us to give up warfare! Many persons have been murmuring: But how could we give up warfare, with those awful Communists ready to attack us?

The space people have a huge space station which orbits the earth, and which cannot be tracked by radar (another Tesla invention which will be mentioned later.) The reason is because the space station is equipped with extremely delicate instruments which might be damaged by radar. These instruments not only record all words spoken upon the earth, but they also record all thought patterns. The murmurings mentioned above naturally came to the attention of the space people, and they want to know why we are concerned about other nations attacking us when we are free to use the Tesla invention any time we wish. Not only along our own borders, but along all borders, so as to quiet all fears which make for aggression. This invention is not something to be kept secret. On the contrary we must insist that all nations use it for mutual protection.

Although it is called an anti-war machine, it is not, properly speaking, a machine. It is more like a magnetic or polarized curtain of air. For your information a similar protective vibratory curtain has been in operation for thousand of years in certain places on this planet—areas regarded as sacred or holy places. This very weekend, at the time of the Tauras Full Moon, the annual Wesak Festival is being celebrated in the Wesak Valley in Tibet. During this ancient ceremony, performed each year in the Wesak Valley, Gautama, the Buddha comes back to the earth for one day from his present home on the star Sirius. He returns annually to greet his friend and collaborator, the Lord Maitreya, the Christ, together with the assembled Masters of Wisdom who constitute the Spiritual Hierarchy on this planet. The Wesak Valley in Tibet has been guarded through the centuries by an invisible magnetic curtain. No human being ever finds his way into this sacred valley unless he is a person of goodwill, a soul dedicated to the welfare of humanity. According to the Divine Plan for this solar system, the time has now come when this entire globe is to become a Sacred Planet; that is why the space people are here to help us, to bring about a state of heaven on earth, for on a sacred planet there can be no warfare; there cannot even be a consciousness of ill-will in the minds and hearts of the inhabitants.

We have mentioned radar, and it is important that we consider this for a moment. Let us clearly understand that scientists and technicians all over the world have never under-estimated the Tesla inventions. Many scientists regarded them with humble admiration; but alas, very often they have been evaluated in an atmosphere strongly tinged with a lurid green shade of envy. Efforts have been made almost constantly, even during Tesla's lifetime in a physical body, to "grab-off" his ideas and try to copy them—at a handsome profit, of course. Tesla invented genuine radar as a part, a very small functional part, of another invention, the anti-war machine. He never intended that radar should function separately, isolated from the anti-war machine.

After the anti-war machine was rejected, some of the scientific minds of our country tried to develop, from hearsay, a small portion of the original invention. They did not have the necessary facts and the result is radar as we know it today. Scientists admit that it does not work very well. It works just as well as an automobile tire without a wheel; it works as well as an electric light without a light bulb. What more can anybody expect from a fragment of a piece of a machine that was never built?

In 1938 Tesla announced that he had developed a method for interplanetary communication.

When Tesla died in 1943 this country was at war, and his papers were removed from the safe in his room and sealed by government authorities. Nothing more was heard of his work in this country except for the valuable information contained in a biography which was published in 1944—a book entitled Prodigal Genius by John J. O'Neill, then science editor of the New York Herald Tribune. O'Neill has since died. As a reporter, O'Neill had long been an acquaintance of Tesla's, but Tesla had never taken O'Neill into his confidence, because O'Neill did not have a sound background in occult studies. He very much desired to probe the ancient mysteries, to study the philosophy of the East and the Ageless Wisdom, and he recognized Tesla as a man whose mind was more at home on the esoteric plane than on the physical plane. Tesla himself never worked freely in physical matter. His machines were all designed in the ether, for he was completely clairvoyant. He not only designed and molded his machines in etheric substance; but he tested the etheric models and made any adjustments required. He never made any notes, drawings or specifications, for he had the power of instant recall. Only in later years, when he was preparing to shed his physical form, did he write out notes and specifications for the aid of his engineers who would continue his work on the physical plane.

When Tesla died in 1943 O'Neill assumed that the work of the superman was over; he stated that Tesla left no "disciples" to carry on. But Tesla left many disciples; many close associates to whom he entrusted all his important notes, drawings, and secrets. The papers left in his safe were purposely placed there to satisfy idle curiosity. Nothing of importance was allowed to fall into greedy hands. He left complete instructions for the building of **the machine for interplanetary communication. The machine was built after his death and placed in operation in 1950. It will not pick up any broadcasts from radio stations on earth, but is designed to receive broadcasts from space ships, and can be equipped to receive from other planets if that should become necessary. When Tesla left instructions for the building of the machine, he said that some day in the near future space ships would be approaching the earth, and it would be nice to have the machine so that we could talk to the space people.**

After the machine was placed in operation, broadcasts were received frequently from space ships, and then shortly thereafter the space ships landed near the home of the owner of the machine. The space visitors were made welcome, and now they frequently visit and chat with the Tesla engineers. The first space ship which landed was 700 feet in diameter, 300 feet high, with a center tube fifty feet in diameter. It held 24 smaller ships, 75 to 100 feet in diameter, and it came from Venus.

It seems apparent that persons who are contacted by space people are usually assigned to some certain phase of the work—something for which they are equipped. Also their work on behalf of the space people seems to follow a certain pattern determined by the space people themselves. For some reason the Tesla phase of the work is just now beginning. Those involved in this particular project are now being placed in communication with each other, and the space people want the inventions developed—but they want them developed in response to a voiced demand from the earth people. Remember that we have to use our free will to get things accomplished. God will work with us, but He will certainly not work for us.

The space people regret that we sit back and wait for our governments or experts or authorities to thrust some development upon us—just anything at all—from chemical fertilizer to a full-scale war. The space people insist that we search our hearts, ask Divine guidance, determine our needs, demand, and then gratefully receive. Let us demand whatever we need to live as free and joyous children of God! Let us demand whatever we need to carry out the Divine Plan of establishing God's Kingdom on the Planet Earth!

# THE TESLA SCOPE
# FOR SPACE
# COMMUNICATIONS

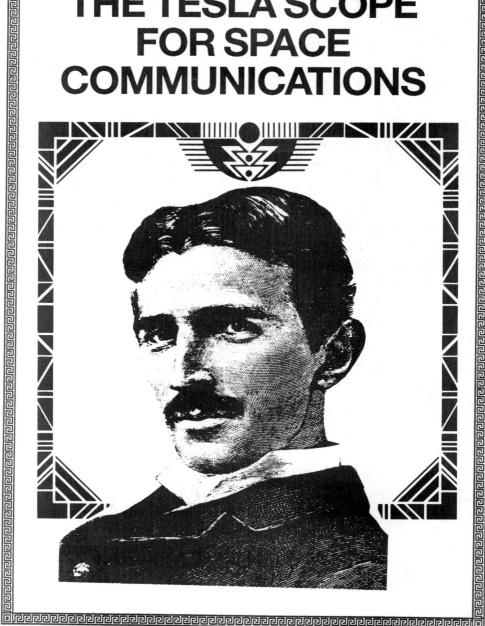

$M$any years ago, long before the days when to many of us the idea of communication with other planets was strictly a Buck Rogers fantasy, Nikola Tesla was already conducting serious research experiments and inventing devices for communication with intelligent life on other planets. Furthermore, he was the first man in Earth's history to record receiving what he firmly believed to be intelligently-controlled signals from outer space.

The page 25 illustration has been copied from a rough sketch (not to scale) drawn by Arthur H. Matthews of the basic concept of the design for a Space Communication Set which would increase the speed of electrical waves to 27 times that of light, as first conceived by Nikola Tesla in 1898, with the objective of communicating with the Planet Venus. Due to pressures of other work, however, the first working model was not built by Tesla until 1918. In 1938, Arthur H. Matthews, under Tesla's guidance, built an improved version of this device at Sanford, in the Province of Quebec, Canada. In 1947, 3 years after Tesla's death, he re-built the Set, incorporating further improvements and finally, in 1967, he re-constructed the Tesla Scope, adapting the new microminiature electronics and reducing its size to 6 ft. long and 4" in diameter. While the more recent models have incorporated the refinements of modern technology, this Space Communication Set retains the same basic concept as originally devised by Nikola Tesla and by this means, Mr. Matthews has, over the years, received messages from space people who claim that they are from Venus.

In the following pages we present a communication from Mr. Matthews regarding these messages:

I am told that the following message purporting to come from Venus, has been transmitted through various channels to the people of Earth for many hundreds of years. It is, in the main, the same message which I have received via the Tesla Scope in the years 1941, 1945, 1947, 1949, 1951, 1957, 1959 and 1961. This same message has been repeated because the same conditions exist on Earth. When I first received it in 1941, I was informed that it came from space people who claimed to be from Venus and who were aboard a spacecraft they called the X-12, a mother-ship 700 ft. in diameter and 300 ft. in height. They told me that if I visualized two saucers put together, with a tube in the centre and a separate ring around the outside, I would have some idea of the shape of this spacecraft which, they stated, carried 24 smaller spaceships inside exactly like the mother-ship except they were from 50 to 100 feet in diameter. They claimed that their spacecraft were operated solely by means of thought waves and that they had no other power—no motors or other forms of propulsion such as Earth people use.

Apart from the omission of certain personal messages connected mainly with my continued work for Tesla on Earth, the following is the message I first received in 1941 and which, in essence, has been repeated over the years.

"When you first receive this message, you will, like most Earth people, doubt. This is one of the strange things we find about the people of

Earth—their continued doubting. They say they believe in God, but they doubt. They say God can cure their sicknesses and their troubles, but they doubt. Therefore, we expect you to doubt also. You will wonder if we really come from Venus—do we come from outer space? And you will wonder how we are able to talk to you in your own language. We use English at this time because you, our friend Matthews, only understand this language, but we have made a study of every language used by mankind. Actually, we would prefer to transmit our thoughts by the use of mental waves which would activate the Tesla machine.

"As we look down on Earth, we note the greatest confusion and misunderstanding. Instead of acknowledging the One God and looking towards Him for enlightenment, we find you all over the Earth running hopelessly and helplessly in pursuit of many things you think will increase your personal happiness—and yet you wonder why you continue to suffer. We hear all of you, year after year, asking the same questions: "Why must we suffer? Why do we still have wars, sickness, poverty, famine and death? Why does pure joy always run away faster than we can, so that we can never catch up with it?" The answers to these questions are to be found in the fact that instead of turning upwards to God, your thoughts are earthbound and you judge only by what you see in others around you, the vast majority of whom are sick, unhappy and full of bad habits, doubting the existence of the Supreme Being and futilely, you follow the group. Your Earth is full of hate and misery and this condition has come to be accepted as the rule for mankind on Earth. This is not how God intended life to be on your beautiful planet, but very few of you obey the Laws of God. Many of you attend some form of religious service on your Sundays, but how many Earth people carry out God's Laws in their everyday lives? We are amazed and saddened to find how much of your time is devoted to inventing and using destructive machines with which you murder each other. We see you spending vast sums of money pretending to bring peace on Earth, when you should know that the only way of obtaining peace is *free*—through Christ Love—there is no other way, so why waste your money and energy? We ask this question realizing that most Earth people have known for almost 2,000 years that the only way to secure peace on Earth and goodwill towards your fellow-men is by following the teachings of Jesus Christ whom a God of Love sent to your planet to bring spiritual enlightenment to mankind.

"Therefore, we can only sadly conclude that the Earth people must be suffering from some form of mental sickness which can only be cured in one way—the way of the Christ Philosophy of Love. You have heard all this before and much of what we say will fall on deaf ears, but our thoughts are directed to those few of the Earth people who have sufficient mental and spiritual power to think clearly and to know right from wrong. These few have been implanted among you to help others to evolve spiritually and to grow in a manner to be of service to the Great, All-Knowing, All-Loving God and all His creatures. Your present behavior is the reason for the continued visits to Earth by those of the space people who endeavour to act as spiritual guardians to your planet, but we must warn you

# THE TESLA SCOPE FOR SPACE COMMUNICATION

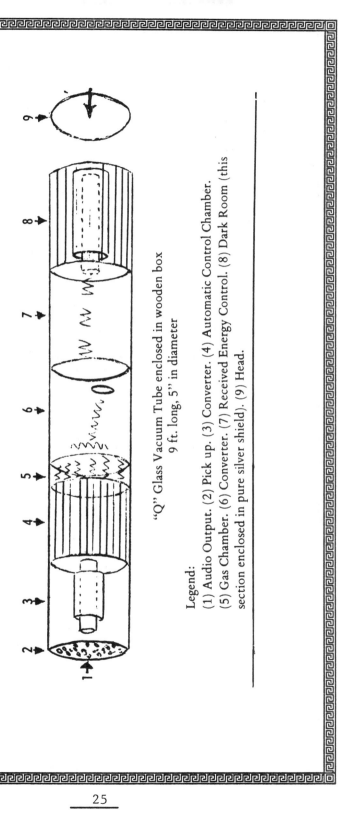

"Q" Glass Vacuum Tube enclosed in wooden box
9 ft. long, 5" in diameter

Legend:
(1) Audio Output. (2) Pick up. (3) Converter. (4) Automatic Control Chamber.
(5) Gas Chamber. (6) Converter. (7) Received Energy Control. (8) Dark Room (this
section enclosed in pure silver shield). (9) Head.

that if you continue to conduct your lives by wrong thinking, you will surely annihilate yourselves—and we shall not have many people to pick up when your Earth is about to be destroyed.

"To help the people of Earth, we brought down one of our own to live among you. During a trip from our planet to Earth, a Venusian child was born. We landed our spacecraft at midnight on July 9, 1856 and decided to leave this boy-child in the care of a good man and his wife. This infant was Nikola Tesla and we left him on Earth in the hope that his higher mental powers and inventive genius would enable him to build advanced machines for the benefit of humanity and that your world, torn by hate and wars, would thereby come out of the darkness into the light. During the years between 1856 and 1943, we landed many times on Earth, but we found no improvement there. At the death of Tesla in 1943, we landed again and attended his funeral. We were saddened to find that the Earth people had used the gifts of Tesla and other great inventors only to satisfy their greed and lust for power, that the same evil conditions existed on Earth and that its people continued to expend their energy on wars and killing their own kind, which is contrary to God's Law which clearly states: Thou shalt not kill.

"These things are beyond our understanding for Venus, in all its history, has never had war. We have but one purpose in life—to serve God and this we do with all our energy of body and mind and because we do this, our mental power grows stronger with age. We remain in perfect health until the day we die. We enjoy perfect harmony, health and happiness with our loved ones all the days of our lives. We have no place in our hearts for selfish desires because we know and believe that God's Law is good and therefore we have no need for man-made laws.

"Lack of faith in God has left your Earth in the Dark Ages and you will never progress or know peace of mind, true happiness and complete harmony until you learn to renew your faith and to become higher in your thinking and living than the crawling things which you now appear to emulate—instead of becoming spiritually-minded beings in the likeness of God. To avert hatred and wars, you must learn to remove every trace of national pride and racial discrimination, for there is, in fact, only one race in the entire Universe—that of mankind whom God created."

In support of Mr. Matthews' words, we would like to present the following condensed extract from "Understanding" (a magazine we can highly recommend), which describes some of Tesla's early experiences with the space communication:

"In the year 1899, Nikola Tesla, with the aid of his financial backer, millionaire J.P. Morgan, set up at Colorado Springs, an experimental laboratory containing high voltage radio transmission equipment, a 200-ft. tower for transmission and reception of radio waves and the best receiving equipment available at that time. One night, when he was alone in the laboratory, he observed what he cautiously referred to as 'electrical actions which definitely appeared to be signals.' The changes were taking place periodically and with such a clear suggestion of number and order that they could not be traced to any cause then known to him. In a written report, Tesla stated: "I was familiar, of course, with such electrical disturbances as are produced by the sun, the Aurora Borealis and earth currents, and I am as sure as I can be of any fact, that these "variations" were due to none of these causes. It was some time afterward, however, that the thought flashed upon me that the disturbances might be due to intelligent control. The feeling is growing constantly upon me that I had been the first to hear the greeting of one planet to another!"

# THE TESLA
# SPACE DRIVE

We recently received a set of plans from a former pupil of Nikola Tesla who believes that a space ship, working on the principles of the "flying saucers," can actually be constructed.

He bases his plans, he told us, upon existing files he secretly obtained shortly before Tesla's death, and before these could be seized by the authorities. He and Tesla had been very close friends and had worked together on a number of projects.

This pupil, however, told us that we must not reveal his name, since his work with the invention is yet in the experimental stages. He also warned us that the principles used in this invention could actually be harmful and very dangerous, considering the "field effect" which he describes as an "anti-electromagnetic field drive."

Although the basic scientific principles are technical, we feel these should be presented to the reader as a matter of record. We have shown this document to a few persons whose scientific knowledge is great, and have been told that the principles advanced in the Tesla Space Drive are sound. They, too, however, warned us of the dangers involved.

The accompanying diagram shows the general arrangement of components in a test device designed to demonstrate the procedure for developing a "one-body system".

Before outlining this procedure I shall explain what I mean by the terms rotation and gyration since both terms appear in the outline to follow and both have very specific meaning for me. In order to understand my use of these terms one

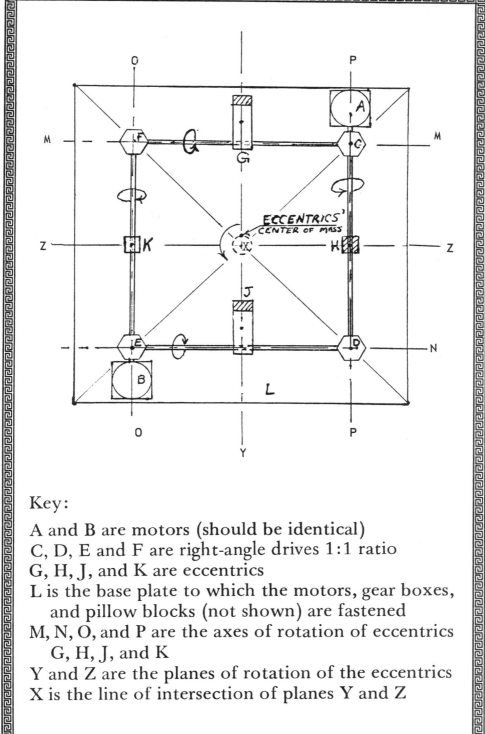

Key:

A and B are motors (should be identical)

C, D, E and F are right-angle drives 1:1 ratio

G, H, J, and K are eccentrics

L is the base plate to which the motors, gear boxes, and pillow blocks (not shown) are fastened

M, N, O, and P are the axes of rotation of eccentrics G, H, J, and K

Y and Z are the planes of rotation of the eccentrics

X is the line of intersection of planes Y and Z

must understand the meanings I attach to them. I do not see gyration as a form of angular motion or rotation but as a form of translatory or linear motion. While gyration simulates rotation it is not true rotation. True rotation is two-dimensional and in order to rotate an object must display radial depth. In a rotating object all component particles travel in circular objects of varying radius about centerpoints lying in a single straight line called the axis of rotation. The range of variation in length of the orbit radii is the radial depth of the object. In the gyrating object (as I think of gyration and use the term) all the component particles again travel in circular orbits. In this case, however, all orbits have the same radius and their centerpoints do not all lie on a single straight line. There is no common axis, no concentricity, and therefore no radial depth.

The first step in developing this system is to cause a counter-clockwise (sense chosen arbitrarily) acceleration of the center of mass of the four eccentrics (refer to diagram) in a circular orbit about the X axis. This must be done without generating a clockwise reaction about the X axis. These conditions can be met by introducing angular acceleration of the eccentrics about their respective axes of rotation, M, N, O, and P. Of course this will produce a gyratory reaction upon the rest of the device but this gyration is also counter-clockwise. Now there is a common point about which the center of mass of the eccentrics and the center of mass of the device as a whole gyrate but these centers are points without radial depth even though they vary in radius of orbit. The center of gyration always lies directly between them. They represent two opposed radii; and because each radius is represented by a point they have no depth.

We have two points traveling in circular orbits about a third point. If we project a straight line through this third point parallel to the X axis we have what I shall call the system axis. The X axis of course is simply the line of intersection of planes Y and Z (refer to Key.). The system axis relates the two components of what I shall call the typically opposed interaction. This is the kind of interaction manifested in this type of "one-body system".

With all components of the system gyrating in a counter-clockwise direction about the system axis we have a SIMULATION of counter-clockwise rotation about this axis with no corresponding clockwise rotation. In the process of creating this situation, however, we have introduced genuine counter-clockwise angular acceleration about the system axis. Referring to the diagram, note the sense of the rotation of the eccentrics about their respective axis and their positions relative to L. The angular accelerations exerted upon H and K produce hub reactions which are linear accelerations toward the right. These accelerations are transmitted by L to the hubs of G and J. The inertial resistance of G and J to these accelerations will of course act in the opposite direction or toward the left and can be represented as forces acting at the centers of mass of these two eccentrics. This means that there is a counter-clockwise force couple acting on both G and J, and these force couples are transmitted to the system as a whole. Therefore the entire system is subject to a counter-clockwise torque about the system axis. There is no corresponding clockwise torque.

The reaction to this angular acceleration is a linear acceleration along the system axis and directed outward from the page. This typically opposed interaction is similar to the one which causes the electron to move about the nucleus of the atom. The electron, however, functions in accordance with the left-hand rule and this system functions in accordance with the right-hand rule.

Although the atomic nucleus is usually passive or inert in the spatial sense, it possesses a latent capacity for regulating its spatial displacement. It takes very special conditions to incite the nucleus to an exercise of this power, but this device sets up those conditions. The nucleus cannot regulate its rate of spatial displacement but it can under certain conditions initiate a change in the directional quality of this displacement. The one-way angular acceleration created by this system causes the nuclei of the system to react. The axial acceleration of the system is really a side-effect caused by the nuclei swerving from their paths in an effort to abolish the field effect caused by the one-way torque. Since they cannot slow themselves down this swerving aside is the only way they can neutralize the effects of the field.

The axial thrust of this device is superimposed upon a wobble-plate effect which is a side-effect of the angular acceleration of the eccentrics about their respective axis. In the positions shown in the diagram the hub reaction initiated by G will thrust its side of L into the page while the hub reaction of J will thrust its side of L out of the page. This produces a torque upon L and the axis of this angular acceleration rotates counter-clockwise about the system axis. As a result this field drive will exhibit a peculiar tendency to wobble noticeably at low thrust levels. This effect fades out, however, as the thrust is increased.

This field drive can be used to propel space-ships. Whether such space-ships would be fit for human habitation, however, or whether they would be deadly I can not say.

## TESLA'S CONCEPTION OF THE EARTH/ATMOSPHERE AS A GIANT ELECTRICAL CAPACITOR

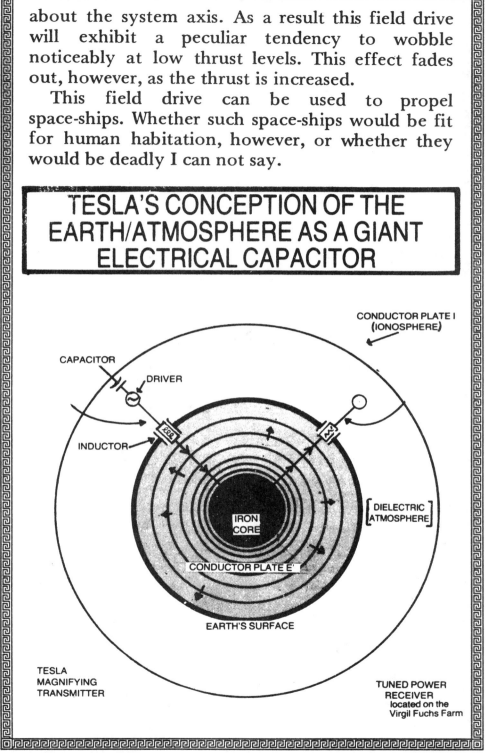

# THE MAN
# WHO COULD
# PHOTOGRAPH
# THOUGHTS

Even in his own day, Nikola Tesla was considered a genius—his accomplishments went way beyond any known form of science. This clipping, from a 1933 edition of the *Kansas City Post,* shows his futuristic mental process.

• • •

PROVING HIS THEORY that a man's efficiency and accomplishments should increase and not diminish with mellow age, Nikola Tesla, inventor, physicist and one of the world's leading electrical technicians, enters his seventy-eighth year busily engaged on three- or four great scientific projects.

Several of these inventions or discoveries will be looked upon as "miracles" by many people, for Mr. Tesla has long been a scientist years ahead of his time, one whose advanced theories have alternately stamped him a "madman" and a wizard.

Just as people ridiculed Copernicus' theory of the planetary system, the unenlightened jeered Tesla's pronouncement, years ago, regarding cosmic rays. The pathfinder and the pioneer—and Mr. Tesla is both—are always condemned by the masses.

NIKOLA TESLA, tall, lean, with the face of an ascetic and deep-set eyes, whose expression denotes concentration on a canvas of work too big for most people's comprehension, partially described a new and inexhaustible source of power he has discovered after years of research, revolutionizing modern physical science. At the same time he touched on his own reservoir of energy which makes such monumental discoveries possible at his advanced age.

How does he tap both these deep wells? What is the secret of fine health, keen mind, unusual vitality and mental force at 77, the time of life when most men are sitting in the sun with shawls over their knees or, alas! lying beneath the sod?

Mr. Tesla is the father of the alternating system of power transmission and radio, the induction motor and Tesla coil.

Asked about his startling new scientific discoveries, one of which concerns the "photographing of thought," which will, he maintains, bring about a tremendous social revolution, he said:

"My first and most important discovery concerns the harnessing of a new source of power, hitherto unavailable, to be developed through fundamentally novel machines of my invention.

"I am not yet prepared to dwell on the details of the project, for they must be checked before my findings can be formally announced. I have worked on the development of the underlying principles for many years. From the practical point of view of the engineer engaged in power development, the first investment will be relatively very great, but once a machine is installed it may be depended on to function indefinitely, and the cost of operation will be next to nothing.

"My power generator will be of the simplest kind —just a big mass of steel, copper and aluminum, comprising a stationary and rotating part, peculiarly assembled. I am planning to develop electricity and transmit it to a distance by my alternating system now universally established. The direct current system could also be employed if the heretofore insuperable difficulties of insulating the transmission lines can be overcome.

"Such a source of power obtainable everywhere will solve many problems with which the human race is confronted. My alternating system has been the means of harnessing 30,000,000 horsepower of waterpower, and there are projects now going on all over the world which will eventually double that amount. But, unfortunately, there is not enough waterpower to satisfy present needs, and everywhere inventors and engineers are endeavoring to unlock some additional store of energy."

WILL THE smashing of the atom lead to this new power energy? Let Mr. Tesla answer:

"The public is naturally led to expect a great revolution through the harnessing of atomic power, but this is an illusion. Atomic energy is not available for work. I operated many years ago apparatus of a capacity of 2,000 horsepower and tension of 18,000,000 volts with which trillions of atoms were smashed in a fraction of a second. I generated all sorts of intense and destructive rays, but found no trace of any energy which should have been liberated through the shattering of atomic structures, according to theory. For the last thirty years I have warned my fellow scientists that there is nothing to be expected in this field except some specific effects due to changes in the atomic structure which may have more or less value."

Beyond adding that the new form of energy which he has been investigating many years would be available at any place in the world in unlimited quantities, and that the machinery for harnessing it would last more than 5,000 years, Mr. Tesla would say little more on the subject. Just when the power will become available for practical purposes he could not predict with any degree of precision. In a few years, perhaps, he ventured to say.

Mr. Tesla then talked of several other projects on which he has been working by way of relief from too much concentration on the main place of work. He described one of his other interests, one highly dramatic, which stirs the imagination and which, doubtless, will sound too revolutionary to most people. But it must not be forgotten, as Mr. Tesla points out, that the ideas of television and radio and airplane were scoffed at in their infancy.

"I expect to photograph thoughts," announced Mr. Tesla calmly, in the same tone of voice that a person occupied with some trivial things in the scheme of life might announce that it was going to rain.

Continued Mr. Tesla: "In 1893, while engaged in certain investigations, I became convinced that a definite image formed in thought must, by reflex action, produce a corresponding image on the retina, which might possibly be read by suitable apparatus. This brought me to my system of television, which I announced at that time.

"My idea was to employ an artificial retina receiving the image of the object seen, an 'optic nerve' and another such retina at the place of reproduction. These two retinas were to be constructed somewhat after the fashion of a checker board, with many separate little sections, and the so-called optic nerve was nothing more than a part of the earth.

"An invention of mine enables me to transmit simultaneously, and without any interference whatsoever, hundreds of thousands of distinct impulses through the ground just as though I had so many separate wires. I did not contemplate using any moving part—a scanning apparatus or a cathodic ray, which is a sort of moving device, the use of which I suggested in one of my lectures of that period.

"Now if it be true that a thought reflects an image on the retina, it is a mere question of illuminating the same properly and taking photographs, and then using the ordinary methods which are available to project the image on a screen.

"If this can be done successfully, then the objects imagined by a person would be clearly reflected on the screen as they are formed, and in this way every thought of the individual could be read. Our minds would then, indeed, be like open books."

BESIDES HIS discoveries concerning the harnessing of the new energy, television and thought photography, Mr. Tesla is working to produce a type of radio transmitter which will insure the strictest privacy in wireless communication regardless of the number of subscribers, and he is developing some important discoveries in molecular physics which will revolutionize the science of metallurgy and greatly improve metals.

After a discussion of his new scientific findings, Mr. Tesla turned to the subject of his personal source of energy and what he considers the real values of life.

"One of the most fundamental and also one of the saddest facts in human life is well brought out in a French proverb which, freely translated, means: 'If youth had the knowledge and age the power of doing,' " said Mr. Tesla. "Our condition of body and mind in old age is merely a certificate of how we have spent our youth. The secret of my own strength and vitality today is that in my youth I led what you might call a virtuous life.

"I have never dissipated. When I was a young man I understood well the significance of that old French proverb, although I doubt that I had even heard it then. But I seemed to have a clear understanding while still young that I must control my passions and appetites if I wanted to make some of my dreams come true.

"So with this in view, quite early in life I set about disciplining myself, planning out a program of living for what I considered the sane and worthwhile life.

"Since I love my work above all things, it is only natural that I should wish to continue it until I die. I want no vacation—no surcease from my labor. If people would select a life work compatible with their temperaments, the sum total of happiness would be immeasurably increased in the world.

"MANY ARE saddened and depressed by the brevity of life. 'What is the use of attempting to accomplish anything?' they say. 'Life is so short. We may never live to see the completion of the task.' Well, people could prolong their lives considerably if they would but make the effort. Human beings do so many things that pave the way to an early grave.

"First of all, we eat too much, but this we have heard said often before. And we eat the wrong kinds of foods and drink the wrong kind of liquids. Most of the harm is done by overeating and underexercising, which bring about toxic conditions in the body and make it impossible for the system to throw off the accumulated poisons.

"My regime for the good life and my diet? Well, for one thing, I drink plenty of milk and water.

"Why overburden the bodies that serve us? I eat but two meals a day, and I avoid all acid-producing foods. Almost everybody eats too many peas and beans and other foods containing uric acid and other poisons. I partake liberally of fresh vegetables, fish or meat sparingly, and rarely. Fish is reputed as fine brain food, but has a very strong acid reaction, as it contains a great deal of phosphorus. Acidity is by far the worst enemy to fight off in old age.

"Potatoes are splendid, and should be eaten at least once a day. They contain valuable mineral salts and are neutralizing.

"I believe in plenty of exercise. I walk eight or ten miles every day, and never take a cab or other conveyances when I have the time to use leg power. I also exercise in my bath daily, for I think this is of great importance. I take a warm bath, followed by a prolonged cold shower.

"Sleep? I scarcely ever sleep. I come of a long-lived family, but it is noted for its poor sleepers. I expect to match the records of my ancestors and live to be at least 100.

"MY SLEEPLESSNESS does not worry me. Sometimes I doze for an hour or so. Occasionally, however, once in a few months, I may sleep for four or five hours. Then I awaken virtually charged with energy, like a battery. Nothing can stop me after such a night. I feel great strength then. There is no doubt about it but that sleep is a restorer, a vitalizer, that it increases energy. But on the other hand, I do not think it is essential to one's well being, particularly if one is habitually a poor sleeper.

"Today, at 77, as a result of well regulated life, sleeplessness notwithstanding, I have an excellent certificate of health. I never felt better in my life. I am energetic, strong, in full possession of all my mental faculties. In my prime I did not possess the energy I have today. And what is more, in solving my problems I use but a small part of the energy I possess, for I have learned how to conserve it. Because of my experiences and knowledge gained through the years, my tasks are much lighter. Contrary to general belief, work comes easier for older people if they are in good health, because they have learned through years of practice how to arrive at a given place by the shortest path."

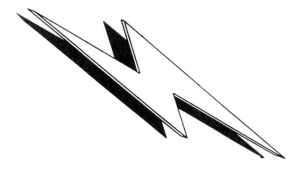

# TESLA'S "COSMIC ENDEAVORS"— HIS OWN STORY

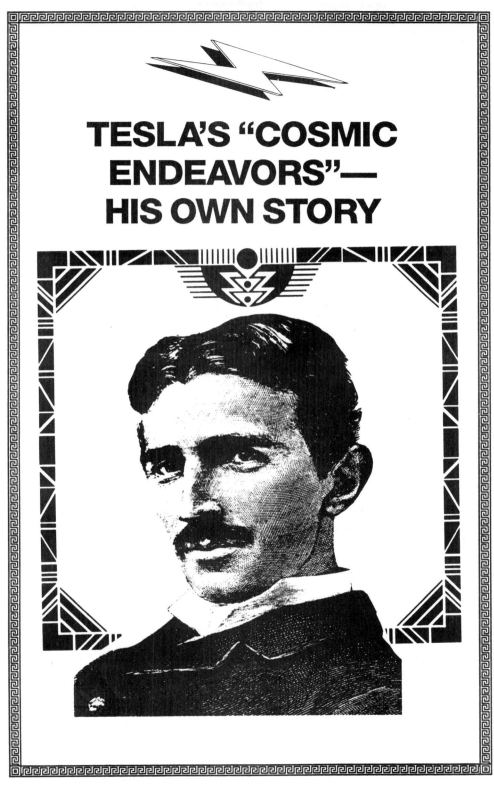

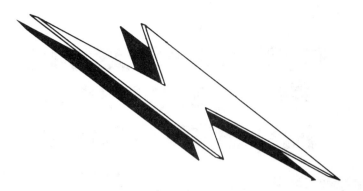

In very guarded words, Tesla once told of his ideas and thoughts of the afterlife, religion and what he referred to as the "Art of Telautomatics." We offer these wise words as proof that Tesla often thought in ways that escaped many other "great thinkers."

• • •

Ever since I was told by some of the greatest men of the time, leaders in science whose names are immortal, that I am possessed of an unusual mind, I bent all my thinking faculties on the solution of great problems regardless of sacrifice. For many years I endeavored to solve the enigma of death, and watched eagerly for every kind of spiritual indication. But only once in the course of my existence have I had an experience which momentarily impressed me as supernatural.

It was at the time of my mother's death. I had become completely exhausted by pain and long vigilance, and one night was carried to a building about two blocks from our home. As I lay helpless there, I thought that if my mother died while I was away from her bedside she would surely give me a sign.

Two or three months before I was in London in company with my late friend, Sir William Crookes, when spiritualism was discussed, and I was under the full sway of these thoughts. I might not have paid attention to other men, but was susceptible to his arguments, as it was his epochal work on radiant matter, which I had read as a student, that made me embrace the electrical career. I reflected that the conditions for a look into the beyond were most favorable, for my mother was a woman of genius and particularly excelling in the powers of intuition. During the whole night every fiber of my brain was stained in expectancy, but nothing happened until early in the morning, when I feel in a sleep, or perhaps a swoon, and saw a cloud carrying angelic figures of marvelous beauty, one of whom gazed upon me lovingly and gradually assumed the features of my mother. The appearance slowly floated across the room and vanished, and I was awakened by an indescribably sweet song of many voices. In that instant a certitude, which no words can express, came upon me that my mother had just died. And that was true. I was unable to understand the tremendous weight of the painful knowledge I receive in advance, and wrote a letter to Sir William Crookes while still under the domination of these impressions and in poor bodily health. When I recovered I sought for a long time the external cause of this strange manifestation and, to my great relief, I succeeded after many months of fruitless effort. I had seen the painting of a celebrated artist, representing allegorically one of the seasons in the form of a cloud with a group of angels which seemed to actually float in the air, and this had struck me forcefully. It was exactly the same that appeared in my dream, with the exception of my mother's likeness. The music came from the choir in the church nearby at the early mass of Easter morning, explaining everything satisfactorily in conformity with scientific facts.

This occurred long ago, and I have never had the faintest reason since to change my views on psychic and spiritual phenomena, for which there is absolutely no foundation. The belief in these is

the natural outgrowth of intellectual development. Religious dogmas are no longer accepted in their orthodox meaning, but every individual clings to faith in a supreme power of some kind. We all must have an ideal to govern our conduct and insure contentment, but it is immaterial whether it be one of creed, art, science or anything else, so long as it fulfills the function of a dematerializing force. It is essential to the peaceful existence of humanity as a whole that one common conception should prevail.

While I have failed to obtain any evidence in support of the contentions of psychologists and spiritualists, I have proved to my complete satisfaction that automatism of life, not only through continuous observations of individual actions, but even more conclusively through certain generalizations. These amount to a discovery which I consider of the greatest moment to human society, and on which I shall briefly dwell.

I got the first inkling of this astounding truth when I was still a very young man, but for many years In interpreted what I noted simply as coincidences. Namely, whenever either myself or a person to whom I was attached, or a cause to which I was devoted, was hurt by others in a particular way, which might be best popularly characterized as the most unfair imaginable, I experienced a singular and undefinable pain which, for want of a better term, I have qualified as "cosmic," and shortly thereafter, and invariably, those who had inflicted it came to grief. After many such cases I confided this to a number of friends, who had the opportunity to convince themselves of the truth of the theory which I have gradually formulated and which may be stated in the following few words:

Our bodies are of similar construction and exposed to the same external influences. This results in likeness of response and concordance of the general activities on which all our social and other rules and laws are based. We are automata entirely controlled by the forces of the medium being tossed about like corks on the surface of the water, but mistaking the resultant of the impulses from the outside for free will. The movements and other actions we perform are always life preservative and though seemingly quite independent from one another, we are connected by invisible links.

So long as the organism is in perfect order it responds accurately to the agents that prompt it, but the moment that there is some derangement in any individual, his self-preservative power is impaired. Everybody understands, of course, that if one becomes deaf, has his eyesight weakened, or his limbs injured, the chances for his continued existence are lessened. But this is also true, and perhaps more so, of certain defects in the brain which deprive the automaton, more or less, of that vital quality and cause it to rush into destruction. A very sensitive and observant being, with his highly developed mechanism all intact, and acting with precision in obedience to the changing conditions of the environment, is endowed with a transcending mechanical sense, enabling him to evade perils too subtle to be directly perceived. When he comes in contact with others whose controlling organs are radically faulty, that sense asserts itself and he feels the "cosmic" pain. The truth of this has been borne out in hundreds of instances and I am inviting other students of nature to devote attention to this subject, believing that through combined and systematic effort, results of incalculable value to the world will be attained.

The idea of constructing an automaton, to bear out my theory, presented itself to me early, but I did not begin active work until 1893, when I started my wireless investigations. During the succeeding two or three years a number of automatic mechanisms, to be actuated from a distance, were constructed by me and exhibited to visitors in my laboratory. In 1896, however, I designed a complete machine capable of a multitude of operations, but the consummation of my labors was delayed until late in 1897. This machine was illustrated and described in my article in the *Century* Magazine of June, 1900, and other periodicals of that time and, when first shown in the beginning of 1898, it created a sensation such as no other invention of mine has ever produced. In November, 1898, a basic patent on the novel art was granted to me, but only after the Examiner-in-Chief had come to New York and witnessed the performance, for which I claimed seem unbelievable.

I remember that when later I called on an official in Washington, with a view of offering the invention to the Government, he burst out in laughter upon my telling him what I had accomplished. Nobody thought then that there was the faintest prospect of perfecting such a device. It is unfortunate that in this patent, following the advice of my attorneys, I indicated the control as being effected through the medium of a single circuit and a well-known form of detector, for the reason that I had not yet secured protection on my methods and apparatus for individualization. As a matter of fact, my boats were controlled through the joint action of several circuits and interference of every kind was excluded. Most generally I employed receiving circuits in the form of loops, including condensers, because the discharges of my high-tension transmitter ionized the air in the hall, so that even a very small aerial would draw electricity from the surrounding atmosphere for hours.

Just to give an idea, I found, for instance, that a

bulb 12″ in diameter, highly exhausted, and with one single terminal to which a short wire was attached, would deliver well on to one thousand successive flashes before all charge of the air in the laboratory was neutralized. The loop form of receiver was not sensitive to such a disturbance and it is curious to note that it is becoming popular at this late date.

In reality, it collects much less energy than the aerials or a long grounded wire, but it so happens that it does away with a number of defects inherent to the present wireless devices. In demonstrating my invention before audiences, the visitors were requested to ask any questions, however involved, and the automaton would answer them by signs. This was considered magic at the time, but was extremely simple, for it was myself who gave the replies by means of the device.

At the same period another larger telautomatic boat was constructed, a photograph of which is shown in this number of the *Electrical Experimenter*. It was controlled by loops, having several turns placed in the hull, which was made entirely water-tight and capable of submergence. The apparatus was similar to that used in the first with the exception of certain special features I introduced as, for example, incandescent lamps which afforded a visible evidence of the proper functioning of the machine.

These automata, controlled within the range of vision of the operator, were, however, the first and rather crude steps in the evolution of the Art of

Telautomatics as I had conceived it. The next logical improvement was its application to automatic mechanisms beyond the limits of vision and at great distance from the center of control, and I have ever since advocated their employment as instruments of warfare in preference to guns. The importance of this now seems to be recognized, if I am to judge from casual announcements through the press of achievements which are said to be extraordinary, but contain no merit of novelty, whatever. In an imperfect manner it is practicable, with the existing wireless plants, to launch an aeroplane, have it follow a certain approximate course, and perform some operation at a distance of many hundreds of miles.

A machine of this kind can also be mechanically controlled in several ways and I have no doubt that it may prove of some usefulness in war. But there are, to my best knowledge, no instrumentalities in existence today with which such an object could be accomplished in a precise manner. I have devoted years of study to this matter and have evolved means, making such and greater wonders easily realizable. As stated on a previous occasion, when I was a student at college I conceived a flying machine quite unlike the present ones. The underlying principle was sound but could not be carried into practice for want of a prime-mover of sufficiently great activity. In recent years, I have successfully solved the problem and am now planning aerial machines devoid of sustaining planes, ailerons, propellers and other external attachments, which will be capable of immense speeds and are very likely to furnish powerful arguments for peace in the near future.

Such a machine, sustained and propelled entirely by reaction, is shown at the end of this chapter, and is supposed to be controlled either mechanically or by wireless energy. By installing proper plants, it will be practicable to project a missile of this kind into the air and drop it almost on the very spot designated, which may be thousands of miles away. But we are not going to stop this. Telautomata will be ultimately produced, capable of acting as if possessed of their own intelligence, and their advent will create a revolution. As early as 1898 I proposed to representatives of a large manufacturing concern the construction and public exhibition of an automobile carriage, which, left to itself, would perform a great variety of operations involving something akin to judgement. But my proposal was deemed chimerical at that time and nothing came from it.

At present many of the ablest minds are trying to devise expedients for preventing a repetition of the awful conflict which is only theoretically ended and the duration and main issues of which I have correctly predicted in an article printed in the *Sun* of December 20, 1914. The proposed League is not a remedy but on the contrary, in the opinion of a number of competent men, may bring about results just the opposite. It is particularly regrettable that a punitive policy was adopted in framing the terms of peace, because a few years hence it will be possible for nations to fight without armies, ships or guns, by weapons far more terrible, to the destructive action and range of which there is virtually no limit. A city, at any distance whatsoever from the enemy, can be destroyed by him and no power on earth can stop him from doing so. If we want to avert an impending calamity and a state of things which may transform this globe into an inferno, we should push the development of flying machines and wireless transmission of energy without an instant's delay and with all he power and resources of the nation.

Order From:
**INNER LIGHT, Box 753,**
**NEW BRUNSWICK, N.J. 08903**

\*    \*    \*    \*    \*

## THE WALL OF LIGHT — NIKOLA TESLA AND THE VENUSIAN SPACE SHIP by A.H. Matthews

Today, the author of this book carries on Tesla's work near his home in Quebec, Canada. Before passing, the great genius gave Matthews a personally written account of his own life which began on a distant planet. Tesla's early life reads like a fairy tale. He was no common mortal. He led a charmed life--given up by doctors at least three times as dead, he was a young man at seventy with a brain that was super keen. Tesla said that he believed he came from Venus, and during the landing of a UFO on the author's property, the members of the ship said Tesla was a child from Venus. As hard as it may be to believe, Matthews also says he was taken on a trip to Mars and given gold rocks by his alien friends. 138 8½x11 pages, stiff binding;    $18.95

\*    \*    \*    \*

# UFOs &
# ELECTROMAGNETISM

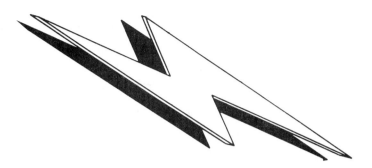

There are many who sincerely believe that Tesla was not of this realm. Some have taken his most secret work and tried to expand on it and develop technology that is truly not of this world. Unfortunately, Tesla is not around to give them a helping hand and so unfortunately, for the most part, these attempts to duplicate an alien technology have not been overly successful.

However, there is said to be in New Zealand a man who has built a flying saucer that can travel at incredible speeds. This vehicle is powered by a revolutionary motor harnessing natural energy from the atmosphere, much like what Tesla was known to be working on in seclusion shortly before his untimely death. This is an incredible project that was first written about in *The Star* of Auckland, New Zealand and it involves a British inventor and a group in New Zealand who are talking about financing him.

The machine would fly from Britain to Auckland in only 39 minutes. According to its New Zealand backers, a spectacular manned test flight is also planned within 8 months if they can raise $20,000. The craft, called a levity disc, is being designed by John Searl of Mortimer in Berkshire. He hopes to demonstrate it at the next Farnborough air show.

Supporters say the levity disc could make rocketry obsolete, because it is:

- Noiseless and pollution-free.
- Requires no runways or launching pads for the vertical takeoff and landing.
- Does not need fuel as it has an "electromagnetic" motor with an energy force field built up to cushion it at supersonic speed.

Aucklander Veronica Comer is the spokesperson for the New Zealand section of Searl National Space Consortium. She told the *Star* this week John Searl and his helpers had made about 41 of the

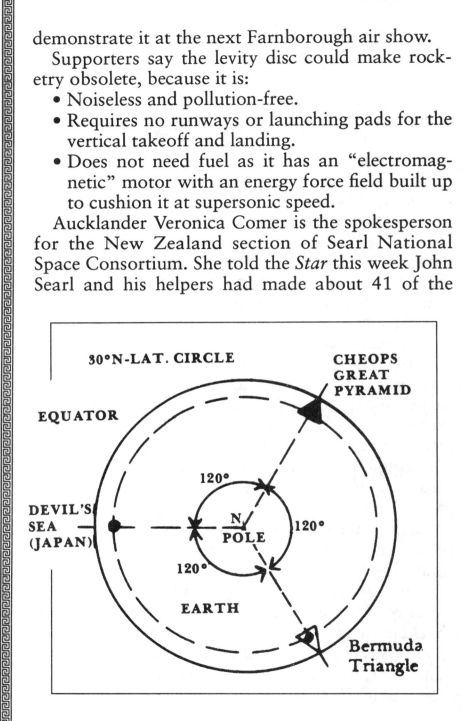

craft, varying in diameter from .9 to 11.5 meters, mostly unmanned, which had flown several hundred times around the world. Mrs. Comer claimed these flights were made secretly before 1971.

"Many governments have shown interest in the Searl effect generator, and he has had the help of NASA in the United States and also the British government which put laboratory facilities at his disposal," she said. "He has just developed and patented a free energy generator for use in motor vehicles under special license..."

Mrs. Comer says Searl has a strong sense of destiny about his vertical disc invention. An engineer, he works around the clock to perfect his craft strenuously resisting huge monetary bids for his patents. On his drawing board, she says, is the design of a massive levity disc, code-named Starship Ezekiel, which he one day hopes to build for interplanetary flight.

## Repeating Dream

Much like Tesla, John Searl was repeatedly plagued by the same terrifying dream when he was a boy. Later he came to realize this was an omen pointing him toward involvement in the realms of cosmic power and space flights.

Searl's dreams revealed exactly how to construct his levity disc, says the Searl National Space Research Consortium's New Zealand spokesperson, Mrs. Veronica Comer.

Scientists scoffed at his layouts and designs. But undeterred, Searl pressed on to the state where he and his supporters firmly believe he'll force a major rethinking in science, magnetism and gravity.

Says Mrs. Comer: "This concept of technology opens a whole wide horizon which must only be for the betterment of the world in general."

And she claims that Searl effect EM energy is under study by the Royal Commission on nuclear power here in New Zealand.

Searl has dedicated his life to bringing his new technology to the world. "All inventors suffer ridicule and opposition and Searl is no exception," says Mrs. Comer.

Searl's work has attracted newspaper publicity and television exposure in Britain, Germany, Japan

and Australia, she adds. It's predicted John Searl will become famous for both his levity disc conception and universal use of his energy concepts.

The following excerpts have been taken from a letter and literature issue by the Consortium to supplement his *Star* article. "A number of physicists joined his team, including a well known professor from the Anti-Gravity Research Institute in Japan, whose technical book, *Principles of Ultra Relativity*, referring in considerable detail to the Searl system was released throughout Japan.

(Reuse of the Searl Effect Generator in motor vehicles: "This should be the forerunner of many such productions, for Free Energy can be used in every field where power or motivation is required, in the home, industry, shipping, mining, freight carrying and all methods of passenger travel. This source of power is inexhaustible and costs nothing.")

## Secret Launch

Searl's "flying saucers" have been secretly launched form a site near Warminster in England, probably giving rise to the UFO reports over a long period in that area. It does not erase the belief that we are being visited from outer space but increases the feasibility of interplanetary travel—for which perhaps we are being programmed.

STARSHIP EZEKIEL will take 2,000 persons, mainly scientists, geologists, astronomers and researchers, medical personnel, passengers and maintenance crew and staff. It will incorporate all the latest materials, components and technologies, will carry no fuel, and travel around the speed of light using *Free Energy*. The cost of constructing this craft will be approximately $24 million. It can stay aloft for 2 years, returning to Earth at intervals for supplies and change of crew.

Searl says that certain persons will stop at nothing to buy out, suppress or eliminate him if he becomes an opposition force on "their scene." He feels he is working under a spiritual cloak of protection as many times he has undergone attack, sabotage, including his family. He has been ridiculed, harangued, nearly driven into the ground both figuratively and literally (by car), but he carries on

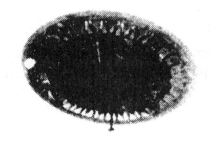

despite all odds.

Like Tesla, he could have been a rich man years ago if he had "given in" to the "system." When various governments would have put untold backing behind him for military research into his concept, but on each occasion he declined for he has utter conviction that this energy source is for the good and progression of mankind and not the destruction of it. For instance, the Arabs in 1973 offered $723 million for his prototype but he declined, feeling it would be used for an evil purpose (against Israel).

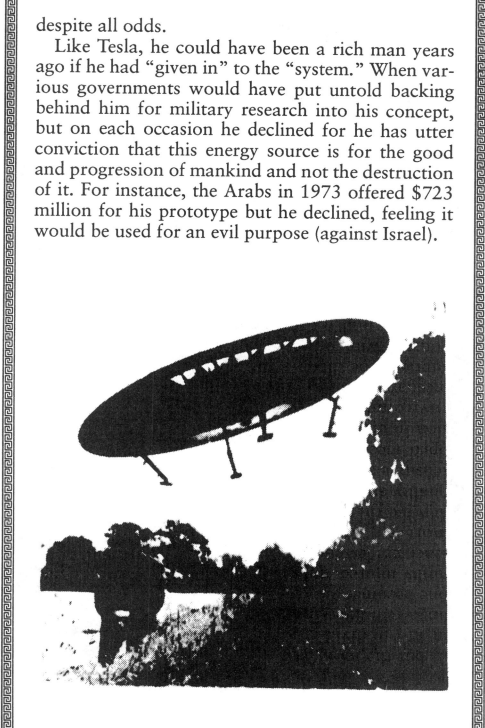

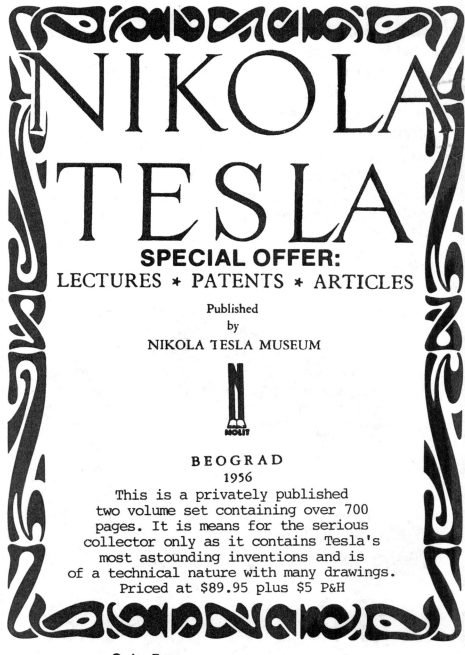

# NIKOLA TESLA

## SPECIAL OFFER:
### LECTURES * PATENTS * ARTICLES

Published
by
NIKOLA TESLA MUSEUM

**BEOGRAD**
1956

This is a privately published
two volume set containing over 700
pages. It is means for the serious
collector only as it contains Tesla's
most astounding inventions and is
of a technical nature with many drawings.
Priced at $89.95 plus $5 P&H